DICTI  !

OF ENGLISH

IDIOMS

VOCABULARY

BUILDING

MANIK JOSHI

<u>Dedication</u>

THIS BOOK IS

DEDICATED

TO THOSE

WHO REALIZE

THE POWER OF ENGLISH

AND WANT TO

LEARN IT

SINCERELY

<u>Copyright</u> <u>Notice</u>

All rights reserved. Please note that the content in this book is protected under copyright law. This book is for your personal use only. No part of this book may be reproduced, stored in a retrieval system, or transmitted, in any form or by any means, electronic, mechanical, recording, or otherwise, without the prior written permission of the author.

Copyright Holder -- Manik Joshi
License -- Standard Copyright License
Year of Publication -- 2014
Email -- manik85joshi@gmail.com

****

<u>IMPORTANT</u> <u>NOTE</u>

This Book is Part of a Series
SERIES Name: "English Word Power"
[A Thirty-Book Series]
BOOK Number: 18
BOOK Title: "Dictionary of English Idioms"
****

Table of Contents

DICTIONARY OF ENGLISH IDIOMS 1

Dedication 2

Copyright Notice 3

Useful English Idioms -- A...6

Useful English Idioms -- B...14

Useful English Idioms -- C...28

Useful English Idioms -- D...33

Useful English Idioms -- E...37

Useful English Idioms -- F...41

Useful English Idioms -- G...46

Useful English Idioms -- H...50

Useful English Idioms -- I 54

Useful English Idioms -- J 56

Useful English Idioms -- K...59

Useful English Idioms -- L 62

Useful English Idioms -- M 65

Useful English Idioms -- N...67

Useful English Idioms -- O...70

Useful English Idioms -- P...73

Useful English Idioms -- Q...76

Useful English Idioms -- R...77

Useful English Idioms -- S 80

Useful English Idioms -- T 86

Useful English Idioms -- U...88

Useful English Idioms -- V...90

Useful English Idioms -- W 92

Useful English Idioms -- XYZ 97

About the Author..98

BIBLIOGRAPHY 99

<u>Useful English Idioms -- A</u>

Aback
be taken aback -- to be shocked

Abeyance
in abeyance -- postponed

Above
above all -- most of all

Abreast
keep abreast of -- to know the latest update

Abstract
in the abstract -- generally

Abundance
in abundance -- in great amounts or quantities

Accident
by accident -- unintentionally

Accompaniment
to the accompaniment of -- in the addition of something else

Accord
in accord -- in agreement
of your own accord -- willingly
with one accord -- in unison

Accordance
in accordance with -- according to a rule or system

Account

by all accounts -- as said by other people

by your own account -- as said by you

of no account -- of no significance

on somebody's account -- because of another person

on account of -- because of

on no account -- without any reason

on your own account -- by or for yourself

on this account -- because of this

turn something to good account -- to make the best use of something

take account of -- to consider something during the decision-making process

Ace

hold all the aces -- to be in the most favorable situation

place your ace -- to use your best argument, etc. to make the situation in your favor

Acquaintance

make the acquaintance of somebody -- to be familiar with somebody for the first time

of your acquaintances -- that you know

on first acquaintance -- on first meeting

Acquire

an acquired taste -- something that you like gradually

Act

act of God -- a natural event

do a vanishing act -- to be absent when you are required to be present

get your act together -- to make your best efforts achieve to your goal

a hard act to follow -- to be the perfect example of something and thus almost impossible to be emulated

in the act of doing something -- while somebody is doing something

in action -- doing the usual activity

into action -- to be implemented

out of action -- not working

Add

add insult to injury -- to aggravate the relationship with somebody

Addition

in addition -- besides

Ado

without further ado -- immediately

Advanced

of advanced age -- very old

Advantage

work to your advantage -- to try to get an advantage to form a particular circumstance

to best advantage -- in a best possible way

turn something to your advantage -- to get an advantage from an unfavorable situation

Advisement

take something under advisement -- to consider something during the decision-making process

Aegis

under the aegis of -- with the support of

Afoul

run afoul of -- to do something illegal

Afar

from afar -- from a long distance away

Afield
far afield -- from a long distance away

Afoul
run afoul of -- to do something illegal

After
after all -- in spite of everything

Age
act your age -- to behave maturely and sensibly
come of age -- to be legally mature
under age -- to be legally immature

Aggregate
in aggregate -- as a total

Agree
agree to differ -- (of two people) to not discuss their different views about something

Aim
take aim at -- to criticize severely

Air
walk on air -- to be delighted
in the air -- felt by many people
on air -- broadcasting on TV, etc.
off air -- not broadcasting on TV, etc.
up in the air -- undecided

Aisle

walk down the aisle -- to get married

Alarm
alarm bells ring -- to be worried and apprehensive in a sudden way

Alive
alive and kicking -- healthy and lively
bring something alive -- to make something exciting
come alive -- to be exciting

And
and all that -- and other things of the same kind
not all that -- not particularly

Allow
allow me -- used to offer help in a polite manner

Allowance
make allowance for something -- to consider something during the decision-making process
make allowance for somebody -- to accept somebody's improper, rude, etc. way of behaving because of special reason

Alone
go it alone -- to do something on your own
leave alone -- to stop annoying somebody
stand alone -- to be independent or unrelated to somebody/something

Along
along with -- in addition to or together with

Altar
on the altar of -- because of something extremely important

Amends
make amends -- to compensate

Amiss
not go amiss -- to be successful
take something amiss -- to unnecessary feel offended

Amok
run amok -- to lose your temper

Amount
any amount of -- a large quantity of
no amount of -- without any effect

Analysis
in the final analysis -- ultimately

Ants
to have ants in your pants -- to be extremely impatient

Ante
raise the ante -- to increase the level of demands or money

Anything
Anything but | not for anything -- certainly not

Apology
make no apology -- to think that you have not done anything wrong, unfair or immoral

Apple
apple of somebody's eye -- that is loved very much
apples and oranges -- totally different from each other

Apron

tied to apron's string -- to be very influenced by somebody | to be controlled by somebody

Arm

cost an arm and a leg -- to be too expensive

keep at arm's length -- to not involve much with somebody

Armed

armed to the teeth -- to have numerous weapons to fight

Arms

be under arms -- to ready to fight with weapons

lay down your arms -- to stop fighting

take up arms -- to get ready to fight

be up in arms -- to be prepared to protest

Arrears

fall in arrears -- to be delayed in paying the owed amount

in arrears -- paid after the work has been finished

As

as against -- on the contrary

as for | as to -- regarding

Ascendant

in the ascendant -- flourishing

Ask

ask for it -- to deserve something unpleasant

don't ask -- used to avoid giving reply to a question

don't ask me -- used to show that you don't know the answer

for the asking -- very easy to get

if you ask me -- according to me

Askance
look askance -- to be suspicious

Astray
go astray -- to get lost | to lose your way

At
be at it again -- to be doing something bad

Auspices
under the auspices of -- with the approval or support of

Avail
of no avail -- of little or no use
to no avail -- without success

Avoid
avoid like the plague -- to completely avoid somebody/something

Awe
stand in awe of -- to respect and be frightened of

Ax (Axe)
have an ax (axe) to grind -- to involve in a situation for a person benefit

<u>Useful English Idioms -- B</u>

Babe
a babe in arms -- a very small baby

Baby
leave somebody holding the baby -- to put your responsibility to others

Back
in the back of your mind -- to be partially aware of something

back to back -- one after the other

behind somebody's back -- without the consent of something

break the back -- to complete the most important, toughest, etc. part of a job

get somebody's back up -- to irritate

get off somebody's back -- to stop irritating somebody

have your back to the wall -- to be forced to do something unpleasant because there is no other choice

on the back of -- as a result of something good

flat on your back -- in bed because of illness

put your back -- to make a great effort

turn your back -- to face in the opposite direction

Backdoor
by the backdoor -- indirectly or unfairly

Backhanded
a backhanded compliment -- insult in the form of admiration

Back seat
take a back seat -- to decide not to play an important role in something

Backwards
Backwards and forwards -- repeated change in the position

Backyard
In your backyard -- near your residence or office

Bad
not bad -- pretty good
too bad -- pity | bad luck

Bag
bag and baggage -- with all your belongings
a bag of bones -- very thin person
be in the bag -- easy to be achieved
leave somebody holding the bag -- to put your responsibility to others
not somebody's bag -- a thing that you don't like or can't do effectively

Balance
hang in the balance -- to be undecided
throw somebody off balance -- to stun somebody

Ball
ball of fire -- extremely enthusiastic person
set the ball rolling -- to initiate
be on the ball -- to be prepared to react instantly

Ballistic
go ballistic -- to be extremely irritated

Bandwagon
jump on the bandwagon -- to be involved for your advantage

Bandy
bandy words -- to argue

Bang

with a bang -- effectively

Banner
under the banner of -- as a part of

Baptism
a baptism of fire -- a tough beginning to an activity or a job, etc.

Bar
behind bars -- in jail
set the bar -- to set a yardstick

Bash
have a bash -- to make an attempt

Basics
go back to basics -- to think about the simplest ideas, rules, etc.

Bat
like a bat out of hell -- with fast speed

Bated
with bated breath -- apprehensively

Battle
the battle lines are drawn -- this is now clear who is supporting which side in a contest, etc.
half the battle -- the most difficult or important part of your goal

Bay
keep at bay -- to defend against

Bead

draw a bead on somebody/something -- to aim at somebody/something in order to shoot them

Beam
off beam -- that is not correct
full of beams -- enthusiastic and lively

Bear
bear fruit -- to be successful
bear heavily on somebody -- something that creates a big problem

Beard
to beard the lion in his den -- to openly say to a powerful person that you disagree with them or you have a different opinion

Bearing
get your bearings -- to try to understand your surroundings
lose your bearings -- to be confused or strayed

Beat
beat about/around the bush -- to talk unnecessarily
beat somebody at their own game -- to unexpectedly perform better than your competitor
beat your breast -- to accept your mistake and feel sorry about it publicly
beat a hasty retreat -- to move fast to avoid something unpleasant

Beck
at somebody's beck and call -- willing to accept somebody's orders

Become
what will become of somebody/something -- what will happen to somebody/something

Bed

not a bed of roses -- not a trouble-free situation

take to bed -- to be very ill and stay in a bed

Bee
the bee's knees -- a perfect thing or person

Beeline
make a beeline for somebody/something -- to go up to somebody/something very fast

Beg
beg leave to do something -- to ask for permission in order to do something

I beg to differ -- used to show your disagreement about something in a polite way

I beg your pardon -- sorry | please repeat

Beggar
beggar description -- that can't be believed easily

Begin
to begin with -- at first or initially | to introduce something

the beginning of the end -- something that initially indicates the end of something else

Behalf
on behalf of -- with a view to helping somebody | because of | instead of

Behavior
be on your best behavior -- to be as politely as you can

Behest
at somebody's behest -- because of somebody's order or request

Bide
bide your time -- wait and see

Bead
draw a bead -- (connected with shooting) to aim carefully at your target

Bearing
take your bearings -- to be assured where you are
lose your bearings -- to be confused

Beeline
make a beeline -- to go straight with fast speed

Behest
at somebody's behest -- at somebody's request

Behove
It behoves somebody to do something -- it is required or justified for somebody to do something

Belabor
belabor the point -- to needlessly repeat something

Belief
Beyond belief -- unbelievable

Better
get the better of -- to gain an advantage | to defeat

Believe
believe it or not -- used to give surprising information
don't you believe it -- used to show untruthfulness
I don't believe it -- used to show irritation or surprise
not believe your eyes/ears -- to be too surprised

Bell
give somebody a bell -- to make a phone call to somebody

Belly
go belly up -- to fail altogether
have had a bellyful of somebody/something -- to have had a too much of something

Belt
below the belt -- an unkind remark
belt and braces -- too cautious or prepared for something
have something under belt -- to have been successful

Bend
bend somebody's ear -- to talk about a problem in detail
bend your mind -- to think a lot about a particular matter
bend the truth -- to say partial truth
on bended knees -- to ask for something in an extremely anxious or polite way

Benefit
give somebody the benefit of the doubt -- to ignore somebody's fault because there is no way to prove it

Bent
bent on doing something -- very eager to do something bad

Beside
be beside the point -- to distract from the main topic
beside yourself -- to be filled with too much of emotions or feelings

Best
your best bet -- the most suitable choice

Betwixt

betwixt and between -- in a middle place

Bib

your best bib and tucker -- best dress for a special occasion

Big

a big cheese -- a very important person in a large community

a big fish -- a very important person in a small community

a big shot -- a very important person

the big picture -- overall condition or situation

give a big hand -- to clap your hands in order to express your approval of somebody

have a big mouth -- too talkative

no big deal -- insignificant

Bill

fit the bill -- to be suitable for something

Bind

In a bind -- in an extremely complicated problem

Bird

the bird has flown -- used to say that somebody has escaped from your clutches

Bit

be in bits -- to be extremely anxious

bit by bit -- gradually or progressively

a bit much -- unfair

bits and pieces -- different sorts of small objects

do your bit -- to fulfill your duty or responsibility

get the bit between your teeth -- to continue doing something with great enthusiasm

not a bit -- not at all; not any

to bits -- into very small pieces

Bitten
be bitten by something -- to be very enthusiastic about something

bite the bullet -- to deal with a very unpleasant situation

bite the dust -- to face defeat

bite the hand that feeds you -- to do something wrong or bad to your supporter or helper

bite your lip -- to control your emotions

bite your tongue -- to prevent yourself from saying something that may offend somebody

Bitter
bitter pill to swallow -- a very unpleasant fact that you have to accept

Black
beat somebody black and blue -- to hit somebody repeatedly and severely

not as black as painted -- not as bad as made out to be

Blast
a blast from the past -- somebody/something from your past that suddenly affects your present

at full blast -- with absolute power

Blaze
blaze a trail -- to set an example

Blessing
blessing in disguise -- an unpleasant-looking situation that ultimately has good effects

Bide
bide your time -- to wait for the appropriate time to take an action

Blind
Turn a blind eye -- to ignore something bad

Blink
In the blink of an eye -- suddenly

Blood
bad blood -- enmity or hatred

make somebody's blood boil -- to irritate somebody

new blood -- a young person

Bolt
a bolt from the blue -- unexpected and surprising event

Boat
be in the same boat -- to be in the same situation, especially unpleasant one

Body
Keep body and soul together -- to manage to survive

Boggle
boggle the mind -- to be unacceptable or unimaginable

Boil
on the boil -- lively and enthusiastic

Bolt
a bolt from the blue -- a strange or surprising event

make a bolt for something -- to run to escape

Bone

a bone of contention -- sticking point that causes serious disagreement

have a bone to pick with somebody -- to want to talk to somebody about an issue of disagreement

Book

by the book -- according to the predefined rules and regulations

in my book -- according to me

Bootstrap

pull yourself up by your own bootstraps -- to make progress on your own

Bow

bow and scrape -- to try to get an advantage from an important person by being very kind to him/her

take your bow -- to bend your head in front of the audience to show them respect

Bottom

lie at the bottom of something -- to be the main cause of something unpleasant

get to the bottom of something -- to discover the main cause of something unpleasant

bottomless pit -- unending or unlimited

Bounds

out of bounds -- unreasonable

Bow

bow and scrape -- to be polite in an exaggerated way to somebody important or powerful

Brain
have something on the brain -- to keep on thinking about something in an unreasonable or unacceptable way

Brew
an evil brew -- a very unpleasant drink made up of unusual things

Brave
put on a brave face -- to show you are confident or pleased when you are not

Break
give somebody a break -- to give somebody an opportunity to show his/her ability

Breath
a breath of fresh air -- new, different and exciting event, person, place or thing, etc.
the breath of life -- the most important part of somebody's existence
speak under your breath -- to speak in a very low voice
take somebody's breath away -- to be amazing

Bridge
bridge the gap -- to lessen the differences between two parties

Brief
in brief -- in a few words

Bright
look on the bright side -- to be optimistic in an unpleasant situation

Broad
In broad daylight -- during daytime

Brunt

bear the brunt of something -- to have to face the most negative effect of something

Bubble

the bubble bursts -- a sudden end to a good-looking situation

Buck

make a fast buck -- to earn a lot of money in a short time

Buff

in the buff -- without wearing any clothes

Bull

a bull in a china shop -- a careless person who acts awkwardly in a serious situation

take the bull by the horns -- to handle a difficult situation.

Bully

bully for you, etc. -- used to show that you are not surprised with somebody's achievement

Bumpy

have a bumpy ride -- to have a tough time

Bunk

do a bunk -- to run away from school, etc.

Burn

burn the candle at both ends -- to be too busy in your job, etc. and don't have time for yourself

burn your fingers -- to suffer unpleasant consequences of your hasty actions

burn the midnight oil -- to work till late night

__burn to the cinders__ -- to badly burn the food

Burst
__burst somebody's bubble__ -- to end expectations of somebody

Bury
__bury the hatchet__ -- to forget your differences

Buy
__buy time__ -- to delay

Buzz
__give somebody a buzz__ -- to make a phone call to somebody

Bygones
__let bygones be bygones__ -- to forget your past disagreements

Useful English Idioms -- C

Cahoots
be in cahoots -- trying to do deceitful act with somebody else

Calm
the calm before the storm -- peace before sudden violent activity

Candle
cannot hold a candle to somebody/something -- not as good as somebody/something else

Candy
like taking candy from a baby -- too easy to do

Canvas
In a canvas -- in a tent

Capitol
make capitol out of something -- to take advantage of a situation

Cards
hold all the cards -- to be in the position of advantage because everything is in your favor
hold cards close to your chest -- to don't tell about your plans
put your cards on the table -- to tell about your plans

Carrot
the carrot and the stick approach -- to decide to reward or punish somebody in order to make them do something

Carry
carry all before you -- to be successful all the time

Cart

put the cart before the horse -- to do something in the order which is incorrect

Case

In any case -- regardless

Cat

let the cat out of the bag -- to carelessly tell something that should be kept secret

play a cat-and-mouse game with somebody -- to keep on changing your way of behaving with somebody, especially in an unexpected way

Catch

catch somebody's eye -- to attract the attention of somebody

catch somebody red-handed -- to catch somebody while they are doing something wrong

Caution

throw/cast caution to the wind -- to not acknowledge the seriousness of the situation

Ceremony

without ceremony -- in an informal way

Certain

for certain -- without doubt

Chalk

chalk and cheese -- very different from each other

Cheek

turn the other cheek -- to remain calm even in the situation where you are likely to be angry

Chicken

a chicken-and-egg situation -- a situation when you cannot find which one of the two things happens first

Chin

keep your chin up -- to keep your morale high in a difficult situation

take something on the chin -- to not complain about the unpleasant situation

Chink

a chink in somebody's armor -- a weak point in somebody's personality, etc.

Chorus

in chorus -- as a group; simultaneously

Chuck

it's chucking it down -- it is raining heavily

Circle

turn full circle -- to return to the original situation

go round in circles -- to make efforts to achieve something unsuccessfully

Circumstances

under no circumstances -- not at all

Clean

make a clean breast of something -- to confess

Cleft

caught in a cleft stick -- to be trapped in a situation where you cannot take the right actions

Clock
against the clock -- before a particular time
round the clock -- continuously

Clockwork
run like clockwork -- to happen in a planned way

Closed
behind closed doors -- privately

Closet
come out of the closet -- to disclose your embarrassing secrets

Cloud
on cloud nine -- extremely happy
under a cloud -- on suspicion

Cog
a cog in the wheel -- an important person in a company, etc.

Confound
confound it/you -- used to express anger

Conspicuous
conspicuous by your absence -- to be absent in an important meeting, party, etc.

Contention
in contention -- the likelihood of winning something
out of contention -- the impossibility of winning something

Crack
crack the whip -- to use your authority forcefully

Cradle
from the cradle to the grave -- from birth until the end of life

Cramp
cramp somebody's style -- to suppress somebody

Creek
up the creek without a paddle -- in an extremely unpleasant situation

Crimp
put a crimp in something -- to have an unpleasant effect something

Cropper
come a cropper -- to fail completely

Crow
as the crow flies -- in a straight line; directly

Cry
cry foul -- to complain of unfair treatment

Cudgel
cudgel your brain -- to think very seriously
take up the cudgel on behalf of -- to defend strongly

Curry
curry favor -- to try to get an advantage by being very kind to somebody

Cushy
a cushy number -- an easy task or job

Useful English Idioms -- D

Daft
daft as a brush -- extremely stupid

Dagger
look dagger at somebody -- to look at somebody angrily

Daily
your daily bread -- the basic things for a living

Damage
what's the damage -- used to ask the cost of something

Damn
damn with faint praise -- to show your discontent by not behaving in an enthusiastic manner

damn the consequences -- used to show that you are going to do something at any cost without caring of consequences

I'll be damned -- used to show extreme surprise

not give a damn -- to show no importance to something

Damnedest
try your damnedest -- to make your best effort

Damp
a damp squib -- a disappointing incident

Damper
put a damper on something -- to destroy the pleasure, success, etc. of something.

Damsel
a damsel in distress -- a woman who urgently needs help

Dangerous
dangerous ground -- a risky situation

Dangle
leave somebody dangling -- to not tell someone that he/she wants to know

Dash
dash somebody's hopes -- to completely destroy somebody's hopes

Date
to date -- until now

Day
any day now -- soon
carry the day now -- to be successful
day by day -- gradually
from day one -- from the beginning
in this day and age -- in the present world
not have all day -- to not have sufficient time
some day -- in the future
those were the days -- used to show the past days were better than the present days
to the day -- exactly
to this day -- even now

Daunt
nothing daunted -- very confident in an unpleasant or difficult situation

Daze
in a daze -- completely confused

Dead

a dead duck -- a failed plan
dead to the world -- fast asleep

Defy
I defy you/anyone to do something -- to challenge someone for doing something that seems impossible

Demur
without demur -- with full confidence

Dent
make a dent in something -- to decrease the amount of money, etc.

Detriment
to the detriment of -- causing harm to somebody/something
without detriment -- not causing harm to somebody/something

Devour
be devoured by something -- to get too much emotional, etc.

Dice
dice with death -- to do an extremely risky thing that can even cause you death

Dint
by dint of doing something -- by way of something

Disposal
at your disposal -- available for use according to your wishes

Disservice
do somebody a disservice damn -- to spoil the reputation of somebody

Dizzy

the dizzy heights -- a very important or powerful position

Doom

doom and gloom | gloom and doom -- extreme disappointment

prophet of doom -- a predictor of bad happenings

Useful English Idioms -- E

Ear

go in one ear and out the other -- to be forgotten soon

shut your ears to something -- to not listen to something

Early

an early bird -- somebody who wakes up early

Earnest

in earnest -- very sincere

Easy

easy money -- money that somebody gets with a little effort

Eat

eat somebody alive -- to criticize or defeat severely

eat like a horse -- to eat too much

eat your words -- to feel sorry about something you have said

I could eat a horse -- I am very hungry

what is eating him/her, etc.? -- Why is he/she irritated?

Ebb

the ebb and flow -- the repeated change in somebody/something

Edge

be on edge -- to be very nervous

take the edge off something -- to make something less intense

Effect

put something into effect -- to implement

come into effect -- to be implemented

to no effect -- without any successful result

with immediate effect -- instantly

Egg

put all your eggs in one basket -- to depend on one particular thing, action, etc. to achieve your goal

Elbow

give somebody the elbow -- to break a relationship with somebody

Elders

Your elders and betters -- old and experienced people

Element

in your element -- to enjoy yourself very much

out of your element -- to be in a new and difficult situation

Eleven

at the eleventh hour -- at the last moment

End

at the end of the day -- the most significant part of the situation, activity, etc.

in the end -- finally

no end of something -- too much of something

put an end to it all -- to kill yourself

make both ends meet -- to somehow manage to earn for your daily needs

Engrave

be engraved in your heart -- to be unforgettable

Entirety

in its entirety -- as a whole

Escape

make good your escape -- to escape successfully

Essence

of the essence -- extremely important

Etch

be etched on your heart -- to be unforgettable

Even

even now -- in spite of everything; at this moment

even so -- despite that

Event

in any event -- whatever the case may be

in the event of something -- if something happens

in that event -- if that happens

Exception

take exception to something -- to be unhappy about something

with the exception of -- excluding

Exhibition

make an exhibition of yourself -- to behave very badly in public

Explain

explain yourself -- to clarify your way of behaving

Extreme

in the extreme -- completely/greatly

Eye

be all eyes -- to be seeing somebody/something carefully

have eyes in the back of your head -- to be able to notice something completely

have your eye on somebody/something -- to be thinking about something serious with a particular purpose

in front of somebody's eyes -- in the presence of something

in the eyes of the law -- according to law

run an eyes over something -- to quickly examine or inspect something

take your eye of the ball -- to not pay attention to the most important aspect of something any longer

with an eye to something -- having a particular purpose

Useful English Idioms -- F

Face
to lose face -- to lose your respect

Face value
to take something at face value -- to readily believe something

Fact
a fact of life -- an unchangeable and unpleasant situation
facts and figures -- detailed information

Fagged
I can't be fagged -- to be extremely tired that you cannot do something further

Fail
without fail -- reliably

Faint
not have the faintest idea -- to have no clue about something

Fair
by fair means or foul -- ready to use both honest or dishonest methods for achieving something

Faith
in good/bad faith -- knowing that something is correct/wrong

Family
run in the family -- to be a general trait in a particular family or group

Fan
fan the flames -- to aggravate the feelings

Fancy

catch somebody's fancy -- to attract somebody

Far

a far cry -- a new and different experience

far and away -- very much

far and wide -- over a large place

go too far -- to behave unreasonably

so far -- until now

take something too far -- to cross your limits

Fear

without fear or favor -- in a reasonable way

Feast

feast your eyes -- to look at somebody with great pleasure

Feather

a feather in your cap -- a respectful deed that you have done

Feel

feel the pinch -- to not have enough money

not feel yourself -- to be unwell

Fettle

in fine/good fettle -- healthy

Few

few and far between -- infrequent; occasional

Fiddle

be on the fiddle -- trying to get money in an illegal or immoral way

play second fiddle -- to be less important

Fierce
something fierce -- unusual

Fight
fight fire with fire -- to argue or fight your opponent in his/her way
fighting spirit -- to be extremely determined to achieve something
fight a losing battle -- to make efforts for something that is impossible to achieve
fight tooth and nail -- to struggle in a very determined way
fight your own battles -- to achieve something through your own efforts

Figment
figment of somebody's imagination -- a non-existing thing

Figure
become a figure of fun -- to do something ridiculous

Find
find your feet -- to become independent

Fingertip
have something at your fingertips -- to be readily available

Fire
come under fire -- to be criticized severely for wrongdoing
hang fire -- to delay
play with fire -- to do dangerous things

Firm
a firm hand -- strong discipline
stand firm -- to be determined with your ideas, beliefs, etc.

Fish

a fish out of water -- somebody who is completely new and uncomfortable surroundings

neither fish nor fowl -- neither of the two things

Flesh
your own flesh and blood -- your relatives
make your flesh creep -- to fill somebody with disgust

Flex
flex your muscles -- to show your power in order to warn somebody

Flight
take flight -- to flee

Flit
do a moonlight flit -- to quietly leave a rented house at night in order to avoid paying rent

Flog
flog a dead horse -- to make your efforts for idle things
flog something to death -- to repeat something in a boring way

Flower
the flower of something -- the best part of something

Fly
fly high -- to be very successful
fly into a rage -- to be extremely angry
with flying colors -- extremely well

Foam
foam at the mouth -- to be extremely angry

Foggy

not have the foggiest idea -- to have no idea about something

Follow
follow in somebody's footsteps -- to try to be very similar to someone in your family
follow suit -- to do something that somebody else has done

Food
food for thought -- an important idea

Fool
make a fool of somebody -- to make somebody appear silly
make a fool of yourself -- to appear silly

Forbid
god/heaven forbid (that...) -- used to say that something unpleasant will not happen

Forbidden
forbidden fruit -- a prohibited thing that seems very attractive

Further
go further -- to say more about something, especially in a severe way
go no further -- to keep something a secret

Fury
like fury -- with immense power, speed, etc.

Fuss
make a fuss -- to show extreme anger to somebody and complain a tot
not be fussed -- to not care about something

<u>Useful English Idioms -- G</u>

Gallery
play to the gallery -- to try to attract somebody's attention in an exaggerated way

Game
play the game -- to behave honestly

Gauntlet
run the gauntlet -- to be attacked or criticized by the mob
take up the gauntlet -- to be ready to compete
throw down the gauntlet -- to challenge somebody to compete

Gear
get into gear -- to start working efficiently

Get
get there -- to be successful

Ghost
give up the ghost -- to die

Gild
gild the lily -- to ruin the good appearance of somebody by trying to improve it

Gill
to the gills -- totally full

Glance
at a glance -- quickly
at first glance -- initially

Glue

glued to the spot -- unable to move because of fear, surprise, etc.

Gnash

gnash your teeth -- to get extremely angry at your failure to achieve a particular thing, result, etc.

Good

a good few -- several

Gorge

somebody's gorge rises -- to be extremely angry

Grace

fall from grace -- to tarnish your image

with a good grace -- willingly and politely

with a bad grace -- unwillingly and rudely

Grade

make the grade -- to be successful

Grain

go against the grain -- to do something unusual

Grant

take for granted -- to not recognize the real value of something

Grass

not let the grass grow under your feet -- to do your work without any delay

Grapevine

through the grapevine -- through other people in informal ways

Great
great and small -- of all kinds

Greek
it is all Greek to me -- that can't be understood

green
green with envy -- extremely jealous

Grin
grin and bear it -- to accept the unpleasant situations without complaining

Grip
in the grip of something -- suffering great trouble
lose your grip on something -- not able to control the difficult situation
come to grips with something -- able to control the difficult situation

Grit
grit your teeth -- to continue something even in a very difficult situation

Groan
groan under the weight -- used to say that there is an excess of something

Ground
cut the ground from under somebody's feet -- to foil somebody's plan all of a sudden

Guard
be on your guard -- to be ready to face the eventuality

Gun
hold a gun to somebody's head – to use threats to make somebody do something

Gut

have somebody's guts for garters -- to severely punish somebody because you are extremely angry with them

sweat/work your guts out -- to work hard to achieve your aim

Gutser

come a gutser -- to fail at something

Gyp

give somebody gyp -- to cause extreme pain to somebody

<u>Useful English Idioms -- H</u>

Hackles
make somebody's hackles rise -- to make somebody extremely angry
somebody's hackles rise -- to be extremely angry

Hair
make somebody's hair stand on end -- to stun somebody
not turn a hair -- to express no emotions in the situation of surprise

Hale
hale and hearty -- healthy, fit and strong

Hammer
go at it hammer and tongs -- arguing fiercely

Hand
hand in glove with somebody -- involving in illegal activity with somebody
hand in hand -- closely related to something
have your hands full -- to be extremely busy
hold somebody's hand -- to give your support to somebody
out of hand -- unable to control

Handy
come in handy -- to be of use

Hard
hard going -- difficult to understand

Harness
in harness -- doing work after rest
in harness with somebody -- working with others to achieve your aim

Hash

make a hash of something -- to do something very badly

Hat
keep something under your hat -- to not disclose the secret thing
throw your hat into the ring -- to decide to take part in a contest

Haul
haul somebody over the coals -- to severely criticized somebody for wrongdoing

Haywire
go haywire -- to be out of control

Head
can't make head or tail of something -- to be completely unable to understand something
lose your head -- to not behave in a reasonable or sensible way

Heave-ho
give somebody the old heave-ho -- to end a relationship | to expel somebody from the job

Heck
for the heck of it -- just for enjoyment

Hedge
hedge your bets -- to minimize your risks

Heed
pay heed -- to pay attention to somebody/something

Hell
all hell broke loose -- a lot of confusion, noise, etc, especially when it happens suddenly

give somebody hell -- to make life miserable for somebody

Helm
at the helm -- in charge of something (organization, etc.)
take the helm -- to take the charge of something (organization, etc.)

Hem
hem and haw -- to take too long for making a decision or saying something

High
high and dry -- in a very unpleasant or dire situation

Hike
take a hike -- go away!

Hilt
up to the hilt -- as much as possible

Hither
hither and thither -- in different directions

Hog
go the whole hog -- to do something thoroughly

Hoist
be hoisted by your own petard -- to be hurt by your own tricks which were intended to harm somebody else

Hook
by hook or by crook -- using honest or dishonest way

Hooky
play hooky -- to run away from school

Horizon
on the horizon -- that may happen in a little while

Hornet
a hornet's nest -- a situation when many people get angry

Horse
straight from the horse's mouth -- getting information directly from the people involved in a situation

Huddle
go into a huddle with somebody -- to talk about something to somebody in a quiet manner

Hue
hue and cry -- strong public protest or agitation

Huff
huff and puff -- to breath noisily because of tiredness
in a huff -- in a very bad mood

Hysterics
have hysterics -- to be extremely irritated

Useful English Idioms -- I

Ice
break the ice -- to make people feel more comfortable at the party, etc. by saying or doing something
cut no ice -- to have no effect

Ill
ill at ease -- anxious or uncomfortable

Image
be the image of somebody/something -- to be very similar to somebody/something else

Inch
every inch -- wholly
inch by inch -- in a slow and careful way
not budge an inch -- to not change at all

Inside
inside out -- to completely change something

Instance
in the first instance -- as the first part of something

Intent
to/for all intents and purposes -- totally

Interest
in the interest of something -- with a view to achieving something

Interim
in the interim -- meanwhile

Iron

have several irons in the fire -- to be taking part in many activities simultaneously

Isolation

In isolation -- independently or separately

Itchy

have itchy feet -- to be very fond of travel or do something different

Itself

all by itself -- automatically

Useful English Idioms -- J

Jack
a jack of all trades -- a person who does a lot of things but not very adeptly

Jam
be in a jam -- to be in a complicated situation

Jaw
somebody's jaw dropped -- somebody got astonished
the jaws of death -- extremely unpleasant or horrific situation that is very difficult to avoid

Jazz
and all that jazz -- and similar things

Jeopardy
in jeopardy -- in an extremely dangerous situation

Jest
in jest -- as a joke

Jewel
the jewel in the crown -- the most impressive, valuable or significant part of something

Job
do the job -- to be successful in the activities that you are doing
do a good/bad job -- to do something in an effective/ineffective manner

Jog
jog somebody's memory -- to make somebody recall something

Join

join battle -- to begin fighting

join hands -- to work together

Joint

out of joint -- working abnormally or ineffectively

Joke

beyond a joke -- extremely irritating

no joke -- too difficult

make a joke of something -- to not take important things seriously

take a joke -- to not feel bad about the jokes made against you

you must be joking -- used to show astonishment

Jot

not a jot -- not even a small amount of something

Joy

full of the joys of spring -- extremely happy

Jugular

go for the jugular -- to forcefully attack somebody's weak point during a conversation

Jump

be jumping up and down -- to be very annoyed, enthusiastic or infuriated about something

jump through hoops -- to do the complicated things with a view to achieving your goal

jump the gun -- to do something too early

Just

just about -- almost

just like that -- all of a sudden

just now -- recently

just so -- with extreme care

just then -- at that point in time

Justice

bring somebody to justice -- to arrest a criminal and put him/her on trial

<u>Useful English Idioms -- K</u>

<u>Keep</u>

keep at something -- to continue doing something

keep somebody at something -- to make somebody continue doing something

keep away -- to not go near somebody/something

keep back -- to maintain a particular distance | to control your emotions and feelings

keep down -- to bend your body | to oppress somebody

keep from -- to prohibit

keep in -- to control your emotions and feelings

keep off -- to avoid

keep on -- to continue

keep out -- to stay outside | to avoid

keep to -- to stick to

keep yourself to yourself -- to be very reserved/reticent

keep under -- to control somebody

keep up -- to continue making progress

<u>Keeping</u>

in somebody's keeping -- under somebody's care.

in keeping with something -- consistent/compatible with something

out of keeping with something -- not consistent/compatible with something

<u>Kick</u>

kick somebody in the teeth -- to not help somebody when they need it the most

<u>Kick</u>

kick up a fuss -- to make a complaint nosily

kick somebody when they are down -- to harm the defeated person

Kid

handle somebody with kid's glove -- to be very careful when dealing with somebody lest they feel upset

kid/kids' stuff -- to be extremely easy to do

Kill

kill time -- to pass your time doing nothing important

kill two birds with one stone -- to be successful in achieving two things with one action

make a killing -- to make a lot of money in a short time

Kilter

out of kilter -- not working properly

Kind

in kind -- in a similar way

of a kind -- very similar

one of a kind -- distinctive/unique

something of the kind -- similar to something mentioned

Kindly

not take kindly -- to dislike

King

a king's ransom -- a very large sum

Kingdom

blow something to kingdom come -- to explode and destroy something completely

Kith

kith and kin -- close acquaintances, friends and relatives

Knee

bring something to their knees -- to defeat somebody in a battle/war

bring something to its knees -- to ruin a company, system, etc. by affecting it badly

Knife

like a knife through butter -- without problems

put the knife in -- to try to hurt somebody

twist the knife in the wound -- to be extremely unkind towards somebody

on a knife-edge -- extremely worried

Knock

knock somebody dead -- to make somebody feel amazed

knock somebody off their pedestal -- to make somebody lose their respect

Know

before you know where you are -- all of a sudden

know your stuff -- to be an expert on a subject

Knit

knit your brows -- to show emotion by bringing your eyebrows too close together

Useful English Idioms -- L

Lam
on the lam -- escaping from the police

Large
larger than life -- very exciting and confident

Last
In the last resort -- as a final choice/option

Latch
on the latch -- (of a door) closed but not locked

Lather
work yourself into a lather -- to be getting angry unnecessarily
in a lather -- in a nervous or angry state

Laugh
laugh in somebody's face -- to openly show disrespect for somebody
be no laughing matter -- to be a serious issue

Leaf
Take a leaf from somebody's book -- to try to emulate successful people

League
in league with somebody -- making dangerous and secret plans with somebody else

Least
not in the least -- not at all

Leap
by leaps and bounds -- very fast

Leeway

make up leeway -- to get rid of a bad position

Leg-up

give somebody a leg-up -- to assist somebody so that they can improve their position

Lesser

the lesser of two evils -- used to show two unpleasant situations when you choose the lesser one

Liberty

at liberty -- no longer in jail; having full freedom

at liberty to do something -- having the right to do something until you don't break any law

Lick

at a fair lick -- at a full speed

a lick and a promise -- the act of cleaning or washing something fast

lick your wounds -- to get your strength back over a period of time

Lid

keep a/the lid on something -- to not tell the secret

take/blow the lid off something -- to tell the secret

Loggerheads

at loggerheads -- in complete disagreement

Loom

loom large -- to be extremely terrifying and unavoidable

Lump

lump it -- to have to accept something unpleasant

take your lumps -- to accept unpleasant things without complaining

Lurch

leave somebody in the lurch -- to not help somebody when they need you the most

<u>Useful English Idioms -- M</u>

<u>Mad</u>
like mad -- intensely
far from the madding crowd -- in a quiet place

<u>Make</u>
make it -- to succeed
make good -- to be successful
make something of yourself -- to become a successful person
make do with something -- to somehow manage with something
of your own making -- to be yourself responsible for the trouble

<u>Maneuver</u>
freedom of maneuver -- the prospect of changing something

<u>Mend</u>
mend your ways -- to stop behaving in an unreasonable way

<u>Mettle</u>
on your mettle -- fully prepared for the test

<u>Mickey</u>
take the Mickey out of somebody -- to make fun of somebody; to mock

<u>Microcosm</u>
in microcosm -- on a small scale

<u>Mill</u>
go through the mill -- to have a difficult time
put somebody through the mill -- to make somebody have a difficult time

<u>Mince</u>
not mince words -- to frankly say something

Mincemeat

make mincemeat of somebody -- to completely defeat somebody

Miniature

in miniature -- too small

Misery

make somebody's life a misery -- to make somebody feel very sad
put an animal, a bird, etc. out of its misery -- to kill an animal, a bird, etc. because it is suffering from an incurable illness
put somebody out of their misery -- to tell somebody what they want to know and thus causing them unworried

Moon

over the moon -- delighted

Moot

a moot point/question -- disagreement about something

Mothball

in mothball -- not in use

<u>Useful English Idioms -- N</u>

<u>Nail</u>
a nail in somebody'/something's coffin -- something that ends something else in an unpleasant way

<u>Name</u>
in name only -- without having real power

<u>Nasty</u>
a nasty piece of work -- cruel, corrupt, dishonest, unkind, or unpleasant person
get/turn nasty -- to become freighting

<u>Nature</u>
against nature -- immoral or unnatural

<u>Near</u>
your nearest and dearest -- your family members or friends
not nearly -- almost not

<u>Necessarily</u>
not necessarily -- possibly/probably but not definitely

<u>Necessary</u>
a necessary evil -- an unpleasant thing, situation, etc. that you have to accept

<u>Neck</u>
be up to your neck in something -- to have to deal with lots of things
neck and neck -- (in a contest) very close

<u>Neighborhood</u>
in the neighborhood of -- around something in number or quantity

Nerve

be a bundle of nerves -- to be extremely nervous or worried

get on somebody's nerves -- to irritate somebody

have nerves of steel -- able to deal with difficult situations in a calm manner

touch a raw nerve -- to upset somebody by mentioning a particular subject

New

break new ground -- to do something new and extremely important in the field of research, etc.

turn over a new leaf -- to improve your personality

News

be good/bad news -- to be possibly helpful/unhelpful

Nick

in the nick of time -- at the last moment

Night

night and day -- continually

Nine

a nine days wonder -- something that causes excitement for a short time

nine time out of ten (ninety-nine times out of a hundred) -- almost always

Nip

nip something in the bud -- to promptly stop doing something as soon as they start showing unpleasant effects

Nod

have a nodding acquaintances with somebody/something -- to know a little about somebody/something

Noise
make a noise about something -- to make a strong complaint about something

Nook
every nook and cranny -- everywhere

Nose
have your nose in something -- to be very interested in reading something
keep your nose out of something -- to not interfere in something

Note
of note -- of great significance
strike a note of something -- to show a particular type of feelings
take note of something -- to notice something in a serious way

Nothing
have nothing to do with -- to take no interest or have no connection
for nothing -- without giving money
nothing like -- not at all
nothing much -- only a little in value or amount

Now
now and again -- occasionally

Nowhere
get nowhere -- to fail to make progress

Null
null and void -- no longer valid

Nutshell
in a nutshell -- very clearly

Useful English Idioms -- O

Ocean
an ocean of something -- a lot of something

Odd/odds
the odd man out -- a very strange person
be at odds with somebody/something -- to clash or disagree

Odor
be in good/bad odor with somebody -- having or not having somebody's consent or support

Off
off and on -- not regularly; infrequently

Offensive
take the offensive -- to attack somebody before getting attacked by them

Often
every so often -- occasionally

On
on and on -- repeatedly

Once
all at once -- unexpectedly
at once -- instantly
just for once -- as an exception
once and for all -- completely or lastly
once in a blue moon -- hardly ever
once or twice -- a few times
once upon a time -- a very long time ago

One
as one -- together
one and all -- everybody
one or two -- some, a few

Oneself
all by oneself -- without the support of anyone else

Only
only just -- barely, not long ago

Open
be an open secret -- to be known to everybody
keep your eyes open -- to notice something quickly

Operation
come into operation -- to start functioning, to be implemented

Opposed
as opposed to -- in contrast

Opposition
In opposition to -- in disagreement with somebody/something

Or
or so -- approximately

Order
in order to -- with the purpose of
out of order -- not working properly, not arranged properly

Ordinary
out of the ordinary -- different from others

Outset

from the outset -- from the beginning

Over

over against -- in contrast with
over and over -- repetitively

Overboard

go overboard -- too excited
throw somebody/something overboard -- to get rid of useless thing

Overdrive

go into overdrive -- to start working with a lot of effort

Overstep

overstep the line -- to behave inappropriately

Useful English Idioms -- P

Pain
take pains -- to make great efforts

Pale
pale beside to something -- to be less important in comparison with something else

Pan
go down the pan -- to be wasted

Pass
pass muster -- to be good enough

Pay dirt
strike pay dirt -- to suddenly become rich

Peace
make your peace with somebody -- to accept your fault in order to end a dispute or an argument with somebody

Peck
pecking order -- an order of importance; hierarchy

Pedestal
to put somebody on a pedestal -- to think too highly of somebody

Penny
every penny -- the whole sum of money
not a penny -- not a little sum of money

Peril
do something at your own peril -- used to show that there is a risk in doing something

Perish
perish the thought -- used to say that something is unlikely to take place

Perpetuity
in perpetuity -- forever

Pervert
pervert the course of justice -- to create problems for law officers so that they can't find the truth about an illegal act

Pick
pick a fight **with somebody** -- to intentionally start a fierce argument with somebody
pick somebody's pocket -- to quietly steal something from somebody's pocket
pick up speed -- to increase speed

Pickle
in a pickle -- in a very difficult situation

Pique
pique somebody's curiosity -- to make somebody curious about something

Pledge
sign the pledge -- to vow never to drink alcohol

Plunge
take the plunge -- to take an action after careful thought

Pomp
pomp and circumstance -- an impressive ceremony

Post

keep somebody posted about something -- to keep on giving the latest update about something to somebody

Precise
to be more precise -- giving more information about the matter

Proud
do yourself proud -- to achieve something impressive

Prowl
on the prowl -- trying to hunt quietly

Puff
be puffed up with pride -- to be extremely proud
puff and pant -- to take deep and noisy breaths after physical effort

Pull
pull a rabbit out of the hat -- to suddenly find a solution, etc.
pull out all the stops -- to make your best efforts to achieve something
pull the plug on something -- to suddenly end a project, etc.

Pursuance
in pursuance of something -- in order to something

Purview
within/outside the purview of something -- within/outside the scope or limits of something

Push
Push something to the back of your mind -- to decide to forget the unpleasant events, etc.

Putty
putty in somebody's hands -- easily influenced by someone

Useful English Idioms -- Q

Queer

queer somebody's pitch -- to make somebody unable to get something

Question

bring something into question -- to bring something under suspicion

come into question -- to come under suspicion

in question -- doubtful

out of the question -- something that is not worth talking about because it is impossible or prohibited

there is no question of -- something is impossible

a question mark against something -- something is doubtful

Quick

to have a quick temper -- to become angry over small matters

Quid

quids in -- to make a big profit

Quite

on the quite -- in a secret manner

quite a lot -- very much, very many

Useful English Idioms -- R

Rack
rack your brain(s) -- to think deeply or for a long time about something

Rag
from rags to riches -- form being poor or deprived to being super-rich
in rags -- very untidy
lose your rag -- to lose your temper

Rage
be all the rage -- to be very fashionable

Ragged
run somebody ragged -- to make somebody tired

Rain
rain or shine -- whatever happens

Rainy
save for a rainy day -- to save money for a bad time

Raise
raise your hand against somebody -- to hit or try to hit somebody

Rake
rake somebody over the coals -- to criticize somebody severely

Ransom
hold somebody to ransom -- to kidnap somebody for money

Rant
rant and rave -- to complain loudly in order to show anger

Rap
(give sb/get) a rap on the knuckles -- to criticize severely | to be criticized severely

Rapture
be, in, go, into, etc. raptures -- to be very enthusiastic for something

Rate
at any rate -- in any event; whatever happens

Rather
rather than -- instead of

Rattle
rattle somebody's cage -- to irritate somebody

Raw
a raw deal -- unfair treatment

Razor
be on the razor edge -- to be in a difficult or complicated situation where you need to be very careful

Realm
beyond/within the realms of possibility -- impossible/possible

Reach
reach for the stars -- to want to achieve something that seems to be almost impossible

Reap
reap a/the harvest -- to get positive or negative results of your deeds

Reckoning

into/out of the reckoning -- with/without a chance of getting successful

Redemption
beyond redemption -- that cannot be saved

Redress
redress the balance -- to make a situation fair or justified again

Rejoice
rejoice in the name of... -- to have a funny name

Retrospect
in retrospect -- looking back

Rile
be all riled up -- to be irritated

Rivet
be riveted to the spot/ground -- too shocked to move

Romp
romp home/to victory -- to win completion or contest without much effort

Roughshod
ride roughshod over somebody -- to treat somebody ruthlessly

Rout
put somebody to rout -- to defeat somebody without much effort

Ruffle
ruffle a few feathers -- to make people feel angry

Useful English Idioms -- S

Samaritan
a good Samaritan -- a very helpful person

Sardine
packed like sardines -- to be very close to each other in an uncomfortable way

Scent
on the scent of something -- very near to find something
put somebody off the scent -- to prevent somebody from finding something

Scheme
sb's scheme of things -- the way things are organized

Scorn
heap scorn on somebody/something -- to criticize somebody

Scrounge
on the scrounge -- trying to get something from somebody without paying anything

Settle
Settle an old score -- to take revenge

Shade
put somebody/something in the shade -- to be better than somebody/something else

Shell
come out of your shell -- to behave confidently in public life

Shoestring
on a shoestring -- using as little money as possible

Short
get short shrift -- to get little sympathy

Shred
in shred -- badly damaged
tear somebody/something to shreds -- to criticize somebody severely

Side
on the other side of the fence -- on the opposite side
the other side of the coin -- opposite aspect of a particular situation

Skid
be on the skids -- to be in a worse and worse condition
put the skids under somebody/something -- to prevent somebody from getting successful

Slack
cut somebody some slack -- to be less critical of something

Slack
take up the slack -- to carefully manage money or people in an organization

Sling
sling your hook -- Go away!

Slog
slog it out -- to compete in order to find the best, etc.

Slouch
be no slouch -- to be able to do something very well

Slug
slug it out -- to compete in order to find the winner

Sly
on the sly -- secretly

Smithereens
smash something to smithereens -- to destroy something into pieces

Snappy
make it snappy -- to hasten

Sniff
have a good sniff around -- to inspect the place vigilantly
not to be sniffed at -- that can be accepted

Snowball
not have a snowball's chance in hell -- to have no likelihood of something

Soapbox
be on your soapbox -- to express your strong opinions about something

Sob
sob your heart out -- to cry loudly because of deep sorrow

Sore
a sore point -- something that may upset you whenever it is mentioned
stick out like a sore thumb -- unpleasantly noticeable

Soup
from soup to nuts -- from beginning to end
in the soup -- in deep trouble

Spate
in full spate -- (of a river) overflowing

Spick
spick and span -- neat and clean

Spill
spill blood -- to kill or seriously injured somebody
spill the beans -- to tell the secret

Splash
cause a splash -- to cause a lot of excitement

Spout
be up the spout -- to be wrong

Spur
on the spur of the moment -- all of a sudden
win your spurs -- to be very famous

Square
back to square one -- to make no progress and return to the original state

Squeeze
squeeze somebody dry -- to get all the money, etc. from somebody

Steam
run out of steam -- to lose your enthusiasm

Stern
be made of sterner stuff -- to have very strong character; determined or bold

Stew

be in a stew -- to be very angry

let somebody stew in their own juice -- to leave somebody to suffer the bad consequences of his/her deeds

Stir

stir the blood -- to make somebody angry or excited about something

stir your stumps -- to hasten

Stock

on the stocks -- being made

take stock of something -- to carefully think about the current situation

put stock in something -- to have a belief in something

Stoop

stoop so low as to do something -- to not care about morality while doing unpleasant things

Stride

get into your stride -- to do something with more confidence, etc.

put somebody off their stride -- to make somebody lose their attention to something

take something in your stride -- to accept the challenge

without breaking stride -- without stopping

Strut

strut your stuff -- to show how well you can perform in dance, etc.

Sublime

from the sublime to the ridiculous -- from high quality to low quality

Sudden

all of a sudden -- in a surprising way

Swathe

cut a swathe through something -- to destroy a large part of something

Sweet

have a sweet tooth -- to like sugary products too much

Sync

in sync -- compatible

out of sync -- incompatible

System

get something out of your system -- to become unaffected with a particular thing

Useful English Idioms -- T

Tab
Keep close tabs on something -- to keep on watching activities of someone

Tandem
in tandem -- happening together

Tatters
in tatters -- badly spoiled

Teeter
teeter on the brink of something -- very near to an extremely dangerous situation

Tempest
a tempest in a teapot -- extreme worry about an unimportant thing

Tenterhooks
(be) on tenterhooks -- extremely excited or worried about something

Thick
thick and fast -- one after another; quickly

Thrall
in thrall to somebody/something -- completely controlled by somebody

Throes
in the throes of something -- in the middle of a difficult situation

Thumb
thumbs up/down -- liked/disliked; accepted/rejected

Tickle
be tickled pink -- to be very happy

Tickle
tickle somebody's fancy -- to make somebody full of pleasure

Tide
swim with/against the tide -- to show agreement/disagreement
the tide turned -- to be lucky in a sudden way

Tight
a tight spot -- a complicated situation

Time
behind the times -- outdated
from time to time -- occasionally

Toing
toing and froing -- useless activities

Trice
in a trice -- all of a sudden

Trojan
work like a Trojan -- to make a great effort

Trot
on the trot -- one after another

Truant
play truant -- to secretly stay away from school

Turtle
turn turtle -- to overturn

Twiddle
twiddle your thumbs -- to keep on waiting

Useful English Idioms -- U

Umbrage
take umbrage -- to feel disturbed without any good reason

Uncertain
in no uncertain terms -- clearly

Uncrowned
the uncrowned king or queen -- the most important person in an unofficial way

Understand
make yourself understood -- to clearly express your thoughts in another language

Undertone
in an undertone -- in a very low voice

Unearthly
at an unearthly hour -- too early in the morning; before dawn

Ungodly
at an ungodly hour -- too early or too late, not in proper time

Unison
in unison -- collectively

Unknown
an unknown quantity -- a skillful person who has hidden his abilities

Unstuck
come unstuck -- to become separated

Up

up against something -- suffering trouble

up and down -- inconsistently

up and running -- working

up there -- very close to an important situation

Upon

upon you -- *something that is going to happen soon*

Upper

get the upper hand -- *to control the situation in your favor*

Upside

turn upside down -- *to create a lot of confusion*

Upstanding

be upstanding -- *(in a formal situation)* stand up

Uptake

be quick on the uptake -- *to understand something easily*

Usual

as usual -- *normally*

Useful English Idioms -- V

Vacuum
in a vacuum -- to be not connected with somebody/something when you should be

Vain
in vain -- without success; failed

Variance
at variance -- in disagreement

Vengeance
with a vengeance -- unusually greater in degree

Vent
give full vent to something -- to strongly express your anger

Venture
Venture into something -- to do something risky

Verge
on the verge of -- near to the moment when something takes place

Victim
fall victim to something -- to be harmed in a serious way

Victory
romp to victory -- to win without much effort

View
in full view -- completely visible
on view -- on a show for the public
have something in view -- to have an idea in your mind

in view of -- taking into consideration
with a view to -- with the intention of

Villain
the villain of the piece -- troublemaker

Virtue
by virtue of something -- by the way of
make a virtue of necessity -- to get an advantage from something that you are required to do

Voice
give voice to something -- to clearly express your thoughts about an important matter
with one voice -- unanimously; collectively

Useful English Idioms -- W

Wake
in the wake of somebody/something -- following somebody/something

Walk
run before you can walk -- to try to do advanced things before learning basics
walk free -- to leave from court without punishment
walk tall -- to be very proud of something

Walkabout
go walkabout -- to appear to be lost

Wall
off the wall -- strange and funny
up the wall -- crazy

Wane
on the wane -- continually decreasing in the importance, value, etc.

War
a war of words -- strong and bitter argument/disagreement.
be on the warpath -- eager to fight somebody

Warrant
I/I'll warrant (you) -- to assure

Wart
warts and all -- without restraint

Wash
wash your hands of somebody/something -- to decide not to involve in the matter

Watch

Watch your mouth -- to speak carefully

Water

not hold water -- (of argument, etc.) unbelievable

Wavelength

be on the same wavelength -- (of more than one people) to thought in similar ways

Wax

wax and wane -- to keep on increasing or decreasing in the significance, power, etc. over a period of time

Way

be made that way -- to have a particular personality
in a big way -- enormously
in some ways -- to some extent
stay out of somebody's way -- to not involve with somebody
the other way round -- opposite
to my way of thinking -- according to me
on the way out -- no longer fashionable
fall by the wayside -- to be unsuccessful

Weave

weave your magic -- to perform in an attractive way

Weigh

weigh your words -- to say something very carefully

Weight

throw your weight around -- (of a person with authority) to make aggressive efforts to achieve your goal

throw your weight behind something -- to support somebody as much as you can

Well
well and truly -- wholly
do well for yourself -- to be successful

Whack
out of whack -- no longer suitable or correct

Wheels
wheels within wheels -- complicated situation involving numerous processes

Whip
hold the whip hand -- to be in a position of power, control, advantage, etc. over something

Whisker
come within a whisker of something -- to almost do something
by a whisker -- by a small amount

Wink
not have a wink of sleep -- to be unable to sleep

Wipe
wipe off the map -- to destroy completely
wipe the state clean -- to start a relationship afresh

Wire
go right down to the wire -- used to say that the final result will be decided in the end

Wobbly

throw a wobbly -- to get angry all of a sudden

Woe
woe betide somebody | woe to somebody -- used to warn that you might be in trouble because of your actions
woe is me! -- use to show extreme regret, grief, etc.

Wolf
keep the wolf from the door -- to not go hungry
throw to the wolves -- to leave somebody in a problematic situation
a wolf in sheep's clothing -- an enemy who pretends to be your friend

Worst
be your own worst enemy -- to be responsible for your own troubles

Worth
worth your salt -- deserving admiration because you meet the expectations of others

Wring
wring somebody's hand -- to firmly shake your hand with somebody
wring somebody's neck -- used to show extreme anger towards somebody
wring your hands -- to show extreme worry by twisting and squeezing your hands

Wringer
go through the wringer -- to suffer horrific experience

Writ
writ large -- very noticeable or obvious

Wrong

on the wrong side of the law -- having to deal with police because you have involved in an illegal activity

take the wrong way -- to unnecessary feel offended by somebody's remark

Writ

writ large -- easy to understand

Useful English Idioms -- XYZ

Year
put years on -- to make somebody look older than their age
take years off -- to make somebody look younger than their age
year in year out -- every year
never in a hundred years -- not at all; never

Yes
yes and no -- not clear about something

Yet
as yet -- up to the present moment; until now

Yore
of yore -- long time ago

Young
Young at heart -- (of old people) to behave like a younger person

Yourself
be yourself -- to behave in a natural way
by yourself -- on your own
to yourself -- privately

****

About the Author

Manik Joshi was born on January 26, 1979, at Ranikhet, a picturesque town in the Kumaon region of the Indian state of Uttarakhand. He is a permanent resident of the Sheeshmahal area of Kathgodam located in the city of Haldwani in the Kumaon region of Uttarakhand in India. He completed his schooling in four different schools. He is a science graduate in the ZBC – zoology, botany, and chemistry – subjects. He is also an MBA with a specialization in marketing. Additionally, he holds diplomas in "computer applications", "multimedia and web-designing", and "computer hardware and networking". During his schooldays, he wanted to enter the field of medical science; however, after graduation, he shifted his focus to the field of management. After obtaining his MBA, he enrolled in a computer education center; he became so fascinated with working on the computer that he decided to develop his career in this field. Over the following years, he worked at some computer-related full-time jobs. Following that, he became interested in Internet Marketing, particularly in domaining (business of buying and selling domain names), web design (creating websites), and various other online jobs. However, later he shifted his focus solely to self-publishing. Manik is a nature-lover. He has always been fascinated by overcast skies. He is passionate about traveling and enjoys solo travel most of the time rather than traveling in groups. He is actually quite a loner who prefers to do his own thing. He likes to listen to music, particularly when he is working on the computer. Reading and writing are definitely his favorite pastimes, but he has no interest in sports. Manik has always dreamed of a prosperous life and prefers to live a life of luxury. He has a keen interest in politics because he believes it is politics that decides everything else. He feels a sense of gratification sharing his experiences and knowledge with the outside world. However, he is an introvert by nature and thus gives prominence to only a few people in his personal life. He is not a spiritual man, yet he actively seeks knowledge about the metaphysical world; he is particularly interested in learning about life beyond death. In addition to writing academic/informational text and fictional content, he also maintains a personal diary. He has always had a desire to stand out from the crowd. He does not believe in treading the beaten path and avoids copying someone else's path to success. Two things he always refrains from are smoking and drinking; he is a teetotaler and very health-conscious. He usually wakes up before the sun rises. He starts his morning with meditation and exercise. Fitness is an integral and indispensable part of his life. He gets energized by solving complex problems. He loves himself the way he is and he loves the way he looks. He doesn't believe in following fashion trends. He dresses according to what suits him & what he is comfortable in. He believes in taking calculated risks. His philosophy is to expect the best but prepare for the worst. According to him, you can't succeed if you are unwilling to fail. For Manik, life is about learning from mistakes and figuring out how to move forward.

Amazon Author Page of Manik Joshi:
https://www.amazon.com/author/manikjoshi
Email: manik85joshi@gmail.com

BIBLIOGRAPHY

(A). SERIES TITLE: "ENGLISH DAILY USE" *[40 BOOKS]*

01. How to Start a Sentence
02. English Interrogative Sentences
03. English Imperative Sentences
04. Negative Forms In English
05. Learn English Exclamations
06. English Causative Sentences
07. English Conditional Sentences
08. Creating Long Sentences In English
09. How to Use Numbers In Conversation
10. Making Comparisons In English
11. Examples of English Correlatives
12. Interchange of Active and Passive Voice
13. Repetition of Words
14. Remarks In the English Language
15. Using Tenses In English
16. English Grammar- Am, Is, Are, Was, Were
17. English Grammar- Do, Does, Did
18. English Grammar- Have, Has, Had
19. English Grammar- Be and Have
20. English Modal Auxiliary Verbs
21. Direct and Indirect Speech
22. Get- Popular English Verb
23. Ending Sentences with Prepositions
24. Popular Sentences In English
25. Common English Sentences
26. Daily Use English Sentences
27. Speak English Sentences Every Day
28. Popular English Idioms and Phrases
29. Common English Phrases
30. Daily English- Important Notes
31. Collocations In the English Language
32. Words That Act as Multiple Parts of Speech (Part 1)
33. Words That Act as Multiple Parts of Speech (Part 2)
34. Nouns In the English Language
35. Regular and Irregular Verbs
36. Transitive and Intransitive Verbs

37. 10,000 Useful Adjectives In English
38. 4,000 Useful Adverbs In English
39. 20 Categories of Transitional Expressions
40. How to End a Sentence

****

(B). SERIES TITLE: "ENGLISH WORD POWER" *[30 BOOKS]*

01. Dictionary of English Synonyms
02. Dictionary of English Antonyms
03. Homonyms, Homophones and Homographs
04. Dictionary of English Capitonyms
05. Dictionary of Prefixes and Suffixes
06. Dictionary of Combining Forms
07. Dictionary of Literary Words
08. Dictionary of Old-fashioned Words
09. Dictionary of Humorous Words
10. Compound Words In English
11. Dictionary of Informal Words
12. Dictionary of Category Words
13. Dictionary of One-word Substitution
14. Hypernyms and Hyponyms
15. Holonyms and Meronyms
16. Oronym Words In English
17. Dictionary of Root Words
18. Dictionary of English Idioms
19. Dictionary of Phrasal Verbs
20. Dictionary of Difficult Words
21. Dictionary of Verbs
22. Dictionary of Adjectives
23. Dictionary of Adverbs
24. Dictionary of Formal Words
25. Dictionary of Technical Words
26. Dictionary of Foreign Words
27. Dictionary of Approving & Disapproving Words
28. Dictionary of Slang Words
29. Advanced English Phrases
30. Words In the English Language

****

(C). SERIES TITLE: "WORDS IN COMMON USAGE" *[10 BOOKS]*

01. How to Use the Word "Break" In English
02. How to Use the Word "Come" In English
03. How to Use the Word "Go" In English
04. How to Use the Word "Have" In English
05. How to Use the Word "Make" In English
06. How to Use the Word "Put" In English
07. How to Use the Word "Run" In English
08. How to Use the Word "Set" In English
09. How to Use the Word "Take" In English
10. How to Use the Word "Turn" In English

****

(D). SERIES TITLE: "WORDS BY NUMBER OF LETTERS" *[10 BOOKS]*

01. Dictionary of 4-Letter Words
02. Dictionary of 5-Letter Words
03. Dictionary of 6-Letter Words
04. Dictionary of 7-Letter Words
05. Dictionary of 8-Letter Words
06. Dictionary of 9-Letter Words
07. Dictionary of 10-Letter Words
08. Dictionary of 11-Letter Words
09. Dictionary of 12- to 14-Letter Words
10. Dictionary of 15- to 18-Letter Words

****

(E). SERIES TITLE: "ENGLISH WORKSHEETS" *[10 BOOKS]*

01. English Word Exercises (Part 1)
02. English Word Exercises (Part 2)
03. English Word Exercises (Part 3)
04. English Sentence Exercises (Part 1)
05. English Sentence Exercises (Part 2)
06. English Sentence Exercises (Part 3)
07. Test Your English
08. Match the Two Parts of the Words
09. Letter-Order In Words
10. Choose the Correct Spelling

Made in United States
Troutdale, OR
01/06/2024

16738998R00056